SUN BEAR

By Rachel Rose

Minneapolis, Minnesota

Credits

Cover and title page, © MrPreecha/Adobe Stock; 3, © Adi Dharmawan/Shutterstock; 4–5, © phichak/Adobe Stock; 7, © jeep2499/Shutterstock; 8–9, © Lillian/Adobe Stock; 11, © Jonah Goh/Shutterstock; 12–13, © Peter Robinson/Adobe Stock; 14, © last19/Adobe Stock; 15, © wahyu edhie anggono/EyeEm/Adobe Stock; 17, © jeep2499/Shutterstock; 19, © Core/Adobe Stock; 21, © Natalia/Adobe Stock; 22, © pito/Adobe Stock, Dn Br/Shutterstock; 23, © Natalia/Adobe Stock.

Bearport Publishing Company Product Development Team
President: Jen Jenson; Director of Product Development: Spencer Brinker; Managing Editor: Allison Juda; Associate Editor: Naomi Reich; Associate Editor: Tiana Tran; Senior Designer: Colin O'Dea; Associate Designer: Elena Klinkner; Associate Designer: Kayla Eggert; Product Development Specialist: Anita Stasson

Library of Congress Cataloging-in-Publication Data

Names: Rose, Rachel, 1968- author.
Title: Sun bear / by Rachel Rose.
Description: Minneapolis, Minnesota : Bearport Publishing Company, [2024] | Series: Library of awesome animals | Includes bibliographical references and index.
Identifiers: LCCN 2023005355 (print) | LCCN 2023005356 (ebook) | ISBN 9798885099950 (hardcover) | ISBN 9798888221785 (paperback) | ISBN 9798888223109 (ebook)
Subjects: LCSH: Sun bear--Juvenile literature.
Classification: LCC QL737.C27 R6635 2024 (print) | LCC QL737.C27 (ebook) | DDC 599.78--dc23/eng/20230223
LC record available at https://lccn.loc.gov/2023005355
LC ebook record available at https://lccn.loc.gov/2023005356

Copyright © 2024 Bearport Publishing Company. All rights reserved. No part of this publication may be reproduced in whole or in part, stored in any retrieval system, or transmitted in any form or by any means, electronic, mechanical, photocopying, recording, or otherwise, without written permission from the publisher.

For more information, write to Bearport Publishing, 5357 Penn Avenue South, Minneapolis, MN 55419.

Contents

Awesome Sun Bears! 4
The Smallest of Them All 6
High in the Tree Tops 8
Tasty Treats 10
Oh Honey, Honey! 12
Danger! 14
Save the Sun Bear 16
Cub Love 18
Leaving Home 20

Information Station 22
Glossary 23
Index 24
Read More 24
Learn More Online 24
About the Author 24

AWESOME
Sun Bears!

SCRATCH! A sun bear uses its sharp claws to climb up high in a tree. Small but powerful, sun bears are awesome!

SOME SUN BEARS CAN CLIMB ALMOST 130 FEET (40 M) HIGH IN TREES.

The Smallest of Them All

Sun bears are the smallest kind of bears on the planet. They are about half the size of their bigger bear relatives. These bears are further set apart by their coloring. They are black or brown like some other bears, but they have a specially shaped yellow patch on their chests. Some say the fur looks like a rising sun, giving these little bears their name.

> **EACH SUN BEAR HAS A YELLOW SPOT THAT IS A LITTLE DIFFERENT.**

High in the Tree Tops

These little bears are found in the **tropical** forests of Southeast Asia. The many trees there make a perfect home for these great climbers. They pull themselves up to the top using their strong legs. They also have sharp claws that can be almost 4 inches (10 cm) long. Sun bears spend most of their time high up in the branches, even sleeping in trees.

BEING HIGH IN THE TREES KEEPS SUN BEARS SAFE FROM **PREDATORS.**

Tasty Treats

Sun bears catch most of their sleep during the day. These **nocturnal** bears get up at night to search for food. Fortunately, sun bears don't have to go far—they find a lot of their meals in trees. Using their claws, they tear away bark from the branches. Underneath, they find insects and other tasty bugs. *YUM!*

> SUN BEARS ALSO EAT LEAVES, BERRIES, LIZARDS, AND SMALL BIRDS.

Oh Honey, Honey!

A sun bear's favorite food is honey! Once it finds a bee nest, the sun bear licks out the honey. Its 10-inch (25-cm) tongue makes quick work of the sweet liquid. **SLURRRP!** Often, a bear licks up some bees, too, but it doesn't seem to mind getting stung!

SUN BEARS ARE ALSO KNOWN AS HONEY BEARS BECAUSE THEY EAT SO MUCH HONEY.

Danger!

While bee stings are of little concern, a real **threat** to sun bears comes from humans. Some people hunt these animals for their meat and fur. But most of the danger comes from the destruction of the bears' **habitat**. People cut down the forests for wood and to clear land to plant coffee and rubber plants.

A coffee plant

Save the Sun Bear

Scientists believe there are fewer than 1,000 sun bears left in the wild. Thankfully, groups of people are working to **protect** the bears from hunters and people who destroy their forest homes. These groups want to help sun bears **survive**.

SOME GROUPS RESCUE SUN BEARS THAT CAN NO LONGER SURVIVE IN THE WILD.

Cub Love

Sun bears usually live alone. Couples come together only when it is time to **mate**. Then, they part ways. The mother bear makes a nest on the ground to get ready for her little one. After about three to eight months, the mother bear gives birth to a baby called a **cub**. Sun bears typically have just one cub at a time, but sometimes they have two.

Leaving Home

A sun bear cub is born blind, but it can see after a few days. As the baby bear grows, its mother teaches it how to climb and find food. Around the age of three, the little bear is able to take care of itself. It is ready to live on its own among the branches.

SUN BEARS CAN LIVE TO BE ABOUT 30 YEARS OLD.

Information Station

SUN BEARS ARE AWESOME!
LET'S LEARN EVEN MORE ABOUT THEM.

Kind of animal: Sun bears are mammals. Most mammals have fur, give birth to live young, and drink milk from their mothers as babies.

Other bears: There are eight kinds of bears. Sun bears are the smallest. Polar bears are the largest.

Size: Sun bears can grow up to 5 ft (1.5 m) long. That's about the length of a park bench.

SUN BEARS AROUND THE WORLD

WHERE SUN BEARS LIVE

Glossary

communicates shares ideas, thoughts, or feelings with others

cub a baby bear

extinct when a kind of animal has died out completely

habitat a place in nature where an animal lives

mate to come together to have young

nocturnal active mainly at night

predators animals that hunt and eat other animals for food

protect to keep something safe

survive to stay alive

threat someone or something that might cause harm

tropical having to do with the warm areas of Earth near the equator

Index

bees 12, 14
claws 4, 8, 10
cubs 18–20
food 10, 12, 20
habitat 14
honey 12
humans 14, 16

mate 18
mother 18–20, 22
Southeast Asia 8
threat 14–15
tongue 12
trees 4–5, 8, 10, 18, 20

Read More

Easton, Marilyn. *Sun Bear or Polar Bear (Hot and Cold Animals).* New York: Children's Press, 2022.

Rose, Rachel. *Grizzly Bear (Library of Awesome Animals).* Minneapolis: Bearport Publishing Company, 2021.

Learn More Online

1. Go to **www.factsurfer.com** or scan the QR code below.
2. Enter "**Sun Bear**" into the search box.
3. Click on the cover of this book to see a list of websites.

About the Author

Rachel Rose writes books for kids and teaches yoga. She lives in California with her favorite animal—her dog, Sandy.

24